SILVER

The life story of an Atlantic salmon

BY RODERICK L. HAIG-BROWN

ILLUSTRATED BY GORDON ALLEN

LYONS & BURFORD, *PUBLISHERS*

89 90 91 92 93   5 4 3 2 1

Library of Congress Cataloging-in-Publication Data

Haig-Brown, Roderick Langmere, 1908–1976.
    Silver : the life story of an Atlantic salmon / Roderick L. Haig-Brown; illustrated by Gordon Allen.
        p.   cm.
    "Nick Lyons books."
    Reprint. Originally published: London : A & C Black, 1931.
    Summary: Traces the life and experiences of an Atlantic salmon from birth to final catch by a fisherman.
    ISBN 1-55821-051-2 : $15.95
    1. Atlantic salmon—Juvenile literature. [1. Atlantic salmon.
2. Salmon.] I. Title.
QL795.F7H3   1989
597'.55—dc20   89-13164
                                                          CIP
                                                          AC

Printed and bound in the United States of America.

To Master Dickie P.

Dear Dickie,

Some time ago I started to tell you (very briefly, for it was after tea and nearly your bedtime) something of Silver's life story. For a little while you gave me all your attention, and then I'm afraid you were bored.

That seemed rather awful to me, because at that time I was just beginning to think that I might be a writer one day. I knew quite well that the story itself was interesting enough, and it could only be that I was telling it badly. So I decided to write the story and offer it to you in the hope of finding myself more successful with my pen than with my lips.

Here it is. I have tried to make it an interesting story and at the same time I have tried to keep to the truth about salmon and their ways. Probably I have failed in both my objects, but if I have I know that you will let me down lightly and take the book for what it's worth. In any case I hope you'll like it a little, and later on, when you are a salmon fisher yourself, perhaps some parts of it will help you to understand salmon.

Always obediently yours,

R. L. H.-B.

Chelsea, S.W.3

SILVER

A DRIZZLING NOVEMBER DAY, TEN YEARS AGO, SAW THE BEGINNINGS of this story. In a tiny stream, far up amid some of the wildest and most desolate hills in the British Isles, lay two big salmon. They were both of them far too big for the stream really, for their backs often rolled right out of the water, and every move they made disturbed the little ripples on the surface. But these two fish had come to the tiny stream to spawn, and a spawning salmon is far too obstinate and determined in his purpose to be turned from it by any inconvenience so slight as that.

On the bank of the Little Stream, just where the salmon were lying, there was a man stretched full length on the wet grass, watching every move of the fish with a tremendous interest. It was very cold up there in the hills, and the drizzling rain must have wetted him to the skin right through his old tweed coat; but he cared nothing for that, for he loved salmon as some men love their books or their wives, and his whole heart was bound up in the delight of gaining new knowledge of them.

As he watched the movements of the two fish in the tiny stream, his eyes were fairly shining with joy. His body tensed with eagerness when he saw the female quivering and shaking in her efforts to lay her twenty thousand eggs, yet he held himself still as a rock, lest the fish should see him. He watched the male salmon doing his share of the work too, and it was not until the whole business was over and darkness was fast approaching that he made a move. Then he rose and stretched his cramped and frozen limbs. As is the way of men who have lived much alone in the out-of-doors, he spoke to himself: "Two grand fish, and a successful spawning. I wonder if I shall catch any of the salmon that are going to hatch from those eggs?" For a moment or two longer he stood there looking down at the water, then he turned and set off with long strides towards a hot bath, dry clothes and an evening in his favourite arm-chair in front of the fire. And sitting there he dreamed of what would happen to all the thousands of eggs that the beautiful female salmon had left on the gravel of the Little Stream.

That is our concern, too: the story of those eggs, and of one of them in particular. As a matter of fact, it was quite a long time before anything happened at all. The two salmon went down the Little Stream, and left the eggs to be nursed by the rippling waters of the shallows and a fitful winter sun. Queer, delicate little things, these eggs that were to produce great strong salmon; but that is often the case in this world. All through life you will find that beauty and delicacy mean usefulness and efficiency. And then the eggs are assisted in their work by the great rivers, and later on by the mighty sea, which gives the salmon so much of his strength and beauty. If we had been there to examine the eggs every day, we

should have learnt a good deal of what they were gaining from the continued flow of fresh pure water over the shallows, and from the rays of wintry sun that came to them through the rain clouds of the hills. If (as did the man in the old tweed coat) we had come back four or five weeks later and picked up some of the eggs from the gravel, we should have found them beautifully round and of a delicate purple-pink colour; and on many of them we should have seen two little black dots, which we should have known for the eyes of the young salmon.

I'm afraid I don't know just which of all the thousands of eggs was Silver's, but I do know that about fourteen weeks after the eggs were first laid Silver's tail broke through the outside of his egg, for all strong healthy little salmon hatch tail first. And not long after the appearance of his tail, his back broke through the top of the egg, and last of all his head popped out at the other side.

The result of all this activity was a funny little fish with a great big ball hanging down where his tummy should have been, a feathery, transparent tail, and a head that was practically nothing but two huge eyes. A funny little thing, but we're all funny when we first break out into the world, and there's generally a reason for it. The round ball where Silver's tummy should have been was simply the yolk of his egg, and, just like the yolk of a chicken's egg, it was intended to feed him until he grew strong enough to feed himself.

During the next six or seven weeks he did nothing but lie among the stones and gravel at the bottom of the stream, thinking of nothing, and scarcely moving save for a slight fanning of his tiny fins that served to keep a supply of fresh water round him and so give him the oxygen that is as necessary to fish as it is to ourselves. But all the time a change was going on: the yolk was slowly disappearing, and Silver was forming a good pair of jaws that would soon enable him to catch what food he needed. At the end of six or seven weeks he was no longer funny: he was a handsome little fish, and he was gradually beginning to realise that there are better things in the life of a young salmon than lying behind a stone on the bottom of a stream. I think it must have been a little pain, just where the yolk had been, that made him dart out from behind his stone one day and seize a tiny insect that was floating past him down the stream. Whatever was the cause of the movement doesn't matter very much, but the movement itself really meant the beginning of Silver's life. From that time on he was continually darting out to seize little insects that seemed to cure the pain where the yolk had been, until gradually he began to take a definite delight in chasing and catching water insects. And day by day he grew more confident and more hungry, until at last he caught his first water snail.

All this time much the same thing was happening to the other eggs on the shallows. Of course the trout and eels and moorhens had gobbled up a good many of them, but that is exactly why Nature makes the salmon lay so many eggs; and before long, in spite of all the hungry creatures of the stream, there were a great many other little salmon fry among the stones on the bottom. Through the whole of the summer Silver and these brothers and sisters of his kept darting about, just feeding and breathing, and sometimes jumping right out of the water either in excitement or else just to see what the outside world looked like. Most of the stronger ones (Silver was one of them) had drifted a little way downstream of the shallow to a place where the water-cress grew thickly close under the bank, and where they found hundreds of the little fresh-water shrimps that make the best food of all for young salmon. And this is partly why Silver was so big and strong later on in life, for a good start is always half the battle.

The main business of the salmon fry was eating, and after that came growing, and then darting away from danger, but they found time for games of a sort, and the greatest game of all was "Hunting the Water-boatman." You have seen the Water-boatman many times, with his long, narrow, boat-shaped body and his long, thin legs that stick out and work backwards and forwards in sharp little strokes to drive him across the water, just as though he were rowing himself along. As the Water-boatman is a great fighter, the little fish found good sport in trying to catch him and eat him. Some day, if you spend long enough beside a stream with little salmon in it, you will see the whole thing for yourself. Five or six of the little fish get together and pick out some unfortunate Water-boatman. At first they are slow to attack, then they begin to dart up at him, and they keep worrying away at the game until one of his oars is nipped off. And that is really the end of it all, for the Water-boatman without one of his oars becomes an easy prey, and the little fish soon "tear him and eat him." I rather fancy that Silver must have been very good at this game, for he was already the strongest and healthiest of all the little salmon. But though the salmon fry could bully the Water-boatmen, they were not by any means lords of the stream, and this fact was often brought home to them suddenly and unpleasantly.

Their very worst enemies were the trout. Often the half-pounders that lived near the water-cress bed would descend upon them to seize an enjoyable samlet supper; and there was a big black trout with a gigantic mouth and rows of sharp teeth who also lived near the water-cress. He had a nasty habit of dashing suddenly into the middle of a whole bunch of the fry and scooping several at once into his hungry jaws. It wasn't very long before Silver learned that every shadow that fell across the water and every faintest move under the water was a danger signal, and at every danger signal he would scuttle off to the weeds, or dash under a stone. Nature's school is a very hard one, but her pupils learn quickly —after all, you and I would learn every bit as quickly if our schoolmasters and schoolmistresses could do such frightening things to us as Nature does to her pupils. Think of the big black trout that so often chased Silver. If you were swimming under water and a huge whale came and chased you and tried to swallow you, it would be about the same thing: it wouldn't take very long for you to learn to keep out of sight when he was near.

That was the life of the salmon fry all through the sumer—eating and hiding, playing in and out of the water-cress roots, and sometimes jumping right out of the water just for the fun of it. But as summer turned to autumn, and the water grew colder, there were fewer flies floating on the water to be seized by the hungry little fish, and fewer insects in the water to make them dart about. The coldness of the water seemed to dull their senses and make them sluggish, and one by one they disappeared, each hiding behind his favourite stone until spring should come to make the world seem worth while again. Silver's size and strength gave him more energy than the others, and it was some time before the coldness of the water dulled his senses, but at last he too crept under his favourite stone and lay there, scarcely moving all through the winter. Perhaps he was thinking of all that he had learnt and done in the summer, but I doubt it. It is more likely that he lay there without any thoughts or feelings, just sleeping away the winter, as the bears do in Canada.

CHAPTER TWO

TOWARDS THE END OF JANUARY THERE CAME A FEW SOFT DAYS OF lukewarm sunshine, and the birds and beasts of the hills decided that winter was past for another year. Hesitatingly at first, then more confidently, their minds turned to thoughts of spring. The warm-hearted little partridges broke from their coveys and went about in pairs; the old mallard with the bright green neck preened his feathers and remembered what a fine bird he was; a sleek little watervole came out from the bank of the stream, sat up and rubbed his eyes with tiny front paws; and even the old black raven, who lived in the cliffs that look straight over the sea, decided that it was time to croak for the joy of being alive.

The lukewarm sun even filtered through the ripples of the Little

Stream to where Silver was lying, and tickled him in the ribs just hard enough to make him take a little notice of what was going on around him. He felt a bit hungry, but he also felt very drowsy—too drowsy to do anything about it. In fact he felt pretty much as you or I feel when we first wake up after a long night's sleep, and before we smell the bacon cooking for breakfast. It's awfully nice, is lying—in—bed—longer—than—you—ought, but somehow it's not such good fun when the bacon's cooking. And that's exactly what Silver found, though his bacon was only flies and shrimps. Little by little his tummy began to remind him that it was still there, and very empty, and at last he made a feeble little dart from his stone and tried to catch a fly that was floating down. He missed that one, and went back to his stone for a whole day. Then he tried again, and this time he caught the fly, but still he went back to his stone. February came. Spring seemed nearer than ever, and gradually the little excursions from the stone became more and more frequent, as Silver grew hungrier and hungrier with every fly or insect he caught.

By the middle of February he was very active and very hungry—so hungry that one of his expeditions took him up to the shallow where he first broke from his egg, and there he found a glorious feast. The trout were spawning, and I'm afraid they were rather wasting their time, because there were eels there, and little trout, and salmon parr, and even a few dace from the Big Salmon River; and just about as soon as the eggs touched the gravel they were gobbled up. Silver thought it was great fun; and day after day he spent in gobbling up the eggs and dashing away from the big trout when they saw him. He was a magnificent little fish by this time, bigger than the other salmon parr of his year, and more active, and every trout egg he swallowed helped to bring back his condition after the long winter fast. In many ways he was beginning to look like a trout, but more graceful in shape, and with eight marks like finger-prints down each side of him. If you had looked very carefully at him, you would have seen that his tail was more forked than a trout's, and if you had counted them you would have found that he had only twelve scales between the funny little fin near his tail and the faint line that ran all down the side of his body. A trout never has less than fourteen.

During March life went on much as usual in the Little Stream. Of course there were lots of adventures to vary the daily task of finding food. Nature is never at peace; all her children pursue and are pursued day and night, and few of them have more enemies to chase them than the salmon parr. By this time Silver was a great deal too clever to be caught by an old trout, but one day he very nearly lost his chance of growing a silver jacket. He was looking about for something to eat, and he saw what looked like a grey stick standing upright in the gravel. Salmon parr are always inquisitive, and so Silver and two other little fish swam up to investigate. They were almost up to the stick when a shadow moved above the water. All three dived for the nearest stone. There was a quick splash, and only two of them reached the stone. The other was on his way down the long throat of the old heron who lived near the stream. Silver didn't go investigating grey sticks after that. I expect one of the trout told him all about herons, because (as every fisherman knows) trout have very clever brains, even if they are too lazy to go down to the sea and grow silver jackets.

It would take books and books to tell of all the other things that Silver saw—of the bright blue kingfishers that could dive so quickly and seize the trout and salmon fry, of the polecat who used to sit on the flat rock at the bend below the water-cress bed and fish for trout, or of the little water-ousel who used to bob up and down in search of flies along the bank just above Silver's favourite feeding-place. I must hurry over all these things to tell you of the greatest event of Silver's life—the beginnings of his silver jacket.

I've told you already that Silver was very much like a trout, and

perhaps you've been wondering why he's called Silver at all, if that was the case. Well, about the end of March, Silver and many of the other parr began to change the colour of their scales. It was a very little change at first, nothing more than the faintest layer of silver poured over the trout-like spots and the big finger-prints along their sides, but it grew plainer and plainer every day, and just about that time the water that ran over the shallows began to sing. I expect you have often noticed how beautifully water can sing, and how it forces an idea into your brain ever so gently, but ever so firmly. If you haven't yet, you will some day.

The song that the shallows sang to the salmon parr was very short, and, like all songs of the streams and rivers, it was repeated over and over again: "Down to the sea"—four short little words—"down to the sea." Softly at first, but growing stronger and stronger. "Down to the sea, down to the sea," sang the shallows all day long, and little by little the song got into the brains of the salmon parr and made them restless. It got into their tails and fins and every part of their trim little bodies. It made them ten times as lively as before, and they jumped out of the water ten times as often as they had ever done before.

At last there came a day when the song was so strong that they simply had to do something more than just jump about; and though they did not really understand the words, most of them turned downstream and started towards the sea. They went slowly at first, even a little doubtfully, but day by day the song grew in volume and power, and day by day the little fish grew brighter and more silvery until, all of a sudden, they found themselves at the place where the Little Stream joins the Great Salmon River.

Silver was among the very first to start for the sea. All the way down the Little Stream he had feasted upon flies and caddis grubs and anything else that he could catch and eat. He had sen many strange salmon parr by the way, some of them older than himself, yet quite without any sign of silver jackets, others almost ready to start for the sea, and others again so young that they were still really salmon fry rather than salmon parr. And it is worth remembering that in all his travels, and among all the thousands of salmon parr that Silver saw, there was never one quite so big as he was at that time.

So Silver came to the Great Salmon River, and completed the first stage of the first great journey of a life that was to be full of journeying. To begin with it was all very strange and rather frightening. In the Little Stream it had been quite easy to tell where the current flowed fast and

where it flowed gently, for the fast water was always broken. In the River it was not so easy. The surface of the water might be as smooth as glass, yet the current might be flowing faster than the fastest water in the Little Stream. Then, too, the River was so wide and deep, and there were so many backwaters and cross-currents, that Silver often found it very difficult to tell whether he was facing upstream, or downstream, or straight across. And there were so many new dangers to worry a young samlet: great fish that lay like logs in the backwaters, and then, just as one tried to swim over the top of them, thinking that they really were old rotten logs, there would come a swirl and the flash and snap of a pair of nightmare jaws armed with row upon row of sharp curving teeth; that was old Esox Lucius, the pirate of the River, and the terror of any and every fish small enough to slide down those nightmare jaws.

Every bit as dangerous, and almost as terrifying, were the fat, lazy chub who seemed always hungry for a nice little salmon. Silver had a good chance to learn a useful lesson from the fate of one fat old chub. It happened on a beautiful sunny day. He was just lying still and dreaming of all the duns and spinners he would like to catch and eat, when suddenly a bright little flash struck the water above where he lay and started to wobble across the River. Silver decided that here was food, and he was just about to chase the flash, when an old fat chub made a savage rush from his lair, caught it in his jaws and turned to go back under the bank. But he never got back. It seemed as though something had suddenly jerked him almost to the surface of the water, and then let him go in a heavy desperate rush downstream. Something trailed behind him in the water, something that tightened up and dragged him back again when he had gone far enough; and when he was back almost to the place where he had seized the flash, the foolish chub lay gasping on the surface, while a shadow leaned over the water, slipped a net under him and lifted him into the air and on to the bank.

That was Silver's first experience of fishermen and their ways, so he lay very quiet on the bottom of the river while it happened, and afterwards thought a good deal about what he had seen. I don't suppose he thought very sensibly about it, but he certainly wondered why a great fish like the chub should be so easily conquered by the tiny flash, and he quite decided that he himself would never lie still while a shadow leaned over the bank and lifted him out in a landing-net. Shadows mean danger, and all little fish know enough to dash off and hide when one comes along. But, as you will see, he soon had a chance of learning for himself all about what had happened to the chub.

CHAPTER THREE

SILVER SOON FOUND THAT THE GREAT SALMON RIVER HAD LEARNED exactly the same song as its cousin the Little Stream; it sang "Down to the sea, down to the sea" in just the same crooning, appealing tone, but with a deeper, more insistent voice that was far more compelling than the caressing soprano of the Little Stream. Silver, like all little fish, and indeed like all Nature's children, was very obedient, and he kept on swimming down the Great River, until one day he felt the current growing stronger than he had ever known it, and below him he heard the Voice of the River muttering and thundering in a tone that he had never heard before. "Hurry, hurry, hurry," said the thundering voice, very quickly, just like that. Silver felt himself drawn along faster and faster by the current, and suddenly he was right in the middle of the thundering voice, gasping for breath amid a cataract of white bubbles. Down he went through the light of the bubbles, down into darkness, and a moment later he found himself battered and gasping in the still backwater just out of the stream at the foot of the waterfall.

As he lay in the still water trying to collect his wits, Silver noticed that the song of the river had grown far less insistent. He couldn't quite make out what the roar of the falls was saying, but he decided to stay where he was for a little while until he felt less battered.

As soon as he had recovered enough to think about it, he knew that he was hungry, so he decided to find a good feeding-place. He was too wise to swim off carelessly without first scouting for danger from where he lay, and it was just as well that he did so, for a great trout was hovering near the surface of the backwater almost directly above him. Wisely Silver decided not to move. He had never seen such a trout as this: long, thick, heavy and dignified, with a broad green back speckled all over with big black spots—one of those trout that anglers call Aldermen—in fact, I think he was the Mayor, or even the Lord Mayor of all Trout, and to watch him feeding would have been an education for many a two-pound trout, to say nothing of a clumsy little salmon parr. As each fly floated over him there was just the slightest movement of his great broad tail, just the least lift of his head; and a faint ring on the surface of the water was the only indication of what had happened to the fly.

Silver was impressed, and he made up his mind to do his best to imitate the dignity of the Lord Mayor. But he was a respectful little fish, and he moved very carefully out of sight of his Lordship before attempting to imitate him.

His chosen spot was a little downstream, and he settled there, hovering just below the surface. It was a good place, and the flies came over him in a constant stream, sailing along like fragile ships floated by the

gentle current. At first Silver's efforts caused the usual twistings of his body and splashes on the surface, but slowly he improved, until he took a dainty olive dun between his jaws without even the tiniest splash and almost without moving his body. He was so pleased with this that he didn't notice the funny taste of the fly until it suddenly stung him violently in the roof of his mouth and he felt himself jerked off his balance. Like a flash he turned to dart under the bank to safety, but something was holding him back: it seemed as though it must be the fly, which had become firmly stuck in the roof of his mouth. Silver struggled and kicked and squirmed and jumped out of the water and shook his head, but it was no good. He felt that he was growing tired, and he had to swim after the fly, which seemed to be pulling him in towards the far bank. He fought all the way across, jumped out of the water two or three times more, and then lay gasping on his side just as tamely as the chub; almost before he knew what was happening, he felt himself lifted into the air, and he was lying on the grass of the River bank.

A voice came from somewhere near him: "Great Scott, it's a salmon parr. I thought it was a two-pound trout. In all the years I've fished the River I've never seen a parr as big as that." Now if you or I had seen the owner of that voice we should have recognised the man who had watched Silver's father and mother spawning in the Little Stream, and we shouldn't have worried about Silver's fate at all; for this man is such a great fisherman and fine sportsman that he is always known as the "Good Fisherman."

It didn't take the Good Fisherman long to make up his mind about what to do with Silver. He knelt down on the grass, and very quickly and gently he unhooked the tiny fly from Silver's jaw. Then he took a small metal disc from one of his many pockets and clipped it on the silly little fin just above Silver's tail. As soon as this was done he dipped his right hand in the River, picked up Silver and placed him in the River with his head upstream until the cool flow of water revived the little fish, and with a flick of his tail he was gone. The Good Fisherman shook his head with a laugh. "I hope we two meet again later on," he said. "Big healthy parr mean big healthy salmon, and you look like being a Sixty-pounder some day."

Later on, when you're a fisherman yourself, I hope you'll remember the way the Good Fisherman put Silver back in the water, and always put small fish back in the same way. Small trout and salmon parr are delicate little things: if you just throw them back into the river any old how they're almost sure to die. Besides, if the owner of the river is a fisherman, and he sees you doing it, you're not very likely to get another chance to throw a fly on his water.

CHAPTER FOUR

THIS LITTLE ADVENTURE MADE QUITE AN IMPRESSION ON SILVER— for an hour or two! Immediately he felt himself swimming free in the River again he darted away to hide under the bank and lie there collecting his wits. His injuries were not very serious, but they worried him a lot at first. His mouth was very sore, his lungs hurt him whenever he breathed, and the silly little fin just above his tail bothered him. I said that the Good Fisherman clipped a little disc on to this fin (it's called the adipose fin) when he landed Silver, and perhaps you wondered why he did it. The disc was stamped with a letter and some numbers, like this: Z53/4/20. That sounds rather pointless, but there was a good reason for it, just as there is a good reason for most things. The letter Z was the mark of the

Good Fisherman, so that anyone who landed a fish marked with the letter Z would be able to write and tell him about it. The number 53 came next because Silver was the fifty-third salmon parr that the Good Fisherman had marked that year, "4" means April and "20" means the year 1920, the year that Silver went down to the sea for the first time. I don't suppose all this would have compensated Silver for the uncomfortable feeling in his adipose fin even if he had known it, but from then on he was a marked fish, and you will see later on in his story how this method of marking teaches us many things about salmon.

To return to Silver. He lay quietly under the bank for nearly two hours, and at the end of that time he had forgotten all about his adventure, for little fish have even shorter memories than little people for unpleasant things. Besides, he had many other things to think about. The River had started the old song of "Down to the sea, down to the sea," and Silver could wait no longer. For the first time, he wanted to know what it all meant; he felt the blood of his thousands of generations of roving ancestors, the urge of his silver jacket, the mystery of the vast salt waters and the Great Feeding-Grounds that lie somewhere under the edge of the North Pole. Two more days passed in fairly lazy descent—he even stopped to feed—but the restlessness was growing. On the third day he noticed several new kinds of weed on the River bottom, and the water seemed to have a curious bitter taste that was so pleasant that he wanted it to become stronger. He swam a little farther downstream, and all of a sudden the water was flowing upstream instead of down, and it felt quite different from any water that Silver had known before. He felt different himself—stronger, lighter, freer, able to swim faster and think more quickly and more clearly. In all his life nothing had been half so glorious as this, so all the muscles in his little body pulled themselves together and said "Jump for joy," and he jumped head over heels out of the water five or six times; then, as if that were not enough, five or six times more.

And that's where we come to a very difficult question. Can salmon talk or not? Charles Kingsley's salmon talked to Tom when he was a Water-Baby, and in Mr. Fortescue's "Story of the Red Deer" not only salmon, but also salmon parr and salmon smolts talk, and you may be quite sure that I am not going to disagree with the two wise men who wrote these wonderful books—I'm certain that all animals talk, some of them perhaps more than others, but all well enough to understand one another. That doesn't mean that all of them talk with their mouths: some talk with little twitches of their tails and other movements of their bodies, and this is the way fish talk. Silver must have been able to talk at least a little, or many of the wonderful things that he did would have been impossible. It's all rather like believing in fairies. When we are very young we believe in fairies; when we are a little older, and think we are a lot older, we don't believe in them; and when we really are a lot older, we believe in them more than ever, because we know quite well that the world would be a hopeless place to live in if there weren't any fairies.

But Silver wasn't a fairy, and so we mustn't spend time talking about them, however important they are. Silver grew tired of jumping out of the water at last, and decided that perhaps he had better find out what to do next, so he looked round to find someone who could tell him, and the first person he saw was a handsome sea-trout. The sea-trout was very little bigger than Silver, but he felt awfully important, because he had been down to the sea, and Silver hadn't yet. Fortunately Silver was quick enough to see this at once, so he went up to him very respectfully, flipped his tail, showed his silver sides, and jumped out of the water a couple of times, all of which meant, "I'm a salmon smolt now, Silver all over. Could you please tell me where I go next?" And the sea-trout, very pleased to be treated so respectfully, looked as though he knew everything in the world, and said (I don't quite know how): "Well, my little man, you see that long, thin fish over there? That's a salmon kelt. He's been up the

River to spawn, and now he's off to the Great Feeding-Grounds to grow strong again. All you've got to do is to follow him."

Silver and the other smolts thanked the sea-trout very gracefully and politely. There were no end of salmon kelts at the mouth of the River, long, thin fish, but graceful and shapely, and quite bright and silvery again, instead of being red and rather fierce-looking as they had been during the spawning season. For the next few days all the smolts who were ready to go off to the Feeding-Grounds kept well together, and did not stray very far from the kelts. They still fed on any flies or insects that were washed down by the River, but they found the salt water full of strange things that were good to eat, and the greatest discovery of all was the first shoal of sand-eels. It was Silver who found them, swimming along about six feet below the surface, and though none of the smolts had attempted to eat anything so large before, Silver led a charge right into the middle of the shoal. Perhaps it was the salt water that gave them courage, but anyhow they all went in as hard as they could, and swallowed sand-eels till they were ready to burst.

That was how things went on for a little while, with the smolts growing bigger each day and more gracefully shaped and more shinily silver. There were not a great many enemies to bother them at the River-mouth, for they were too small to interest the seals, who killed some of the kelts, and with the exception of the big eels, there were not many fish to bother them just there. But hundreds and hundreds of the smaller ones were killed and eaten by the sea-gulls that are allowed to exist in thousands round the mouths of the rivers. Every year it is the same; all because of a foolish law that says that gulls must never be killed, thousands and thousands of salmon smolts, who might otherwise have lived to become big and valuable salmon, die before they ever see the Great Feeding-Grounds in the North.

But fortunately Silver was too big for the gulls, and at last there came

a day when some of the kelts started on the long northward journey, and with them went the smolts. For days and days they travelled along the coast, always towards the north, and feeding as they went. Often kelts and smolts from other rivers joined them, and once or twice Silver and his fellows lingered a short while to feed at some pleasant river-mouth. But for the most part this great northward journey to the Feeding-Grounds was a steady movement, and daily it grew more purposeful and more determined. Curiously enough, there was really no need at all for Silver and the other smolts to follow the kelts. It seemed as though they had always known the way, and as a matter of fact that was exactly the case. Long before the memory of man, Silver's ancestors had travelled that same route from the River-mouth to the Great Feeding-Grounds, and an instinctive knowledge of the way had been passed down through countless generations of salmon. There are people who sneer at the thing we call heredity, which means the passing on of cleverness, and sometimes actually knowledge, from parents to children; but men who know anything of salmon and other fishes and animals, or of human beings, will tell you that it counts for a very great deal.

But we must not interrupt the story of Silver to talk of these things; there are hundreds of books in which you can read all about them and decide for yourself which of the wise men are really wise and which are writing nonsense. For wise men seldom agree about these things, and they can't all be right, so perhaps some of them are not so wise as we think they are. However that may be, I am sure that Silver could have found his way to the Great Feeding-Grounds without following the kelts, and that hundreds of smolts do so every year.

By this time Silver and all the smolts who had left the River with him had quite decided that they had never known anything even nearly so glorious as the sea. There was an endless store of wonderful food in the sea, and every day they swallowed all they could, and every day they grew and grew. And then the salt water made them feel so much more active and strong than they had felt in the River, and it was very wonderful to jump from the white crest of a wave and plunge back into the heaving green waters of the next one.

Long before they reached the Great Feeding-Grounds the smolts weighed twice as much as when they left the River-mouth, and the kelts had become well-shaped and strong again. Silver thought he had never seen anything so glorious as the sight of one of these great handsome fish leaping a clear three feet from the water and falling back with a mighty splash. He promised himself that he would do the same thing one day, only, like all youngsters, he decided that he would be just a little bit bigger than the biggest and just a little bit handsomer than the handsomest of his elders. And he had a better chance than most youngsters of keeping his promise, for he was one of the chosen among salmon—one of those favoured ones that are born of noble, healthy parents, and leave the river at the end of their first year, having fed always on an ample supply of the best of everything.

Every day that went by taught Silver more of the world. Just as you and I learnt that there was a whole big house outside our nurseries, so Silver learned that there was a water-cress bed below the shallow where he was born. And as we learned of the garden round our house, so Silver learned that the Little Stream ran all the way down to the Great River. To him the discovery of the Great River was what the discovery of Britain is to us when we first realise how large she is. And in the sea Silver found what you will some day find in the great wide world outside the British Isles: people and places and things, so innumerable, all so different, that in a million lives it would only be possible to learn the first beginning of a little bit about it all.

For many days this voyage of discovery led our salmon along the coast, until at last they were beyond the very north of Scotland, farther north even than the Shetland Isles, north of the Faroes, with nothing but the wide Norwegian sea between them and the Great Feeding-Grounds. And on the day that they left the Faroes behind they came upon the first shoal of herring. There is no food anywhere, in all the rivers and all the seas in the world, that salmon love better than herrings. Unfortunately for this particular shoal of herrings, they too were on their way north to the Great Feeding-Grounds, so our salmon just followed them all the way, gorging themselves to the full on the bright little fish whenever they felt hungry.

CHAPTER FIVE

Perhaps I have been a little careless in talking so freely of the Great Feeding-Grounds, for I'm bound to confess that it's difficult to say just where they are. As a matter of fact, no one knows exactly where they are, and it isn't very likely that anyone will find out for a few years yet. Most people agree that they are almost certainly to the north of Iceland, near Greenland, inside the Arctic Circle; but beyond that it all seems rather vague. In any case, it is a world of ice inside the Arctic Circle, and on the land there are very few animals except Polar Bears and Foxes, and very few birds except the Horned Puffins and the Little Auks.

North Polar Region

SVALBARD

GREENLAND

Lappland

ICELAND

NORWAY

SWEDEN

UNITED KINGDOM OF
GT. BRITAIN & N. IRELAND

REP.
OF IRELAND

NORTH ATLANTIC

Newfoundland

OCEAN

G. ALLEN

But in the sea there are hundreds and hundreds of wonderful things: icebergs and whales, seals and sea-lions; salmon to feed the seals, and thousands of herrings to feed the salmon, and millions of little fish to feed the herrings. And when fish like salmon and herrings are tired after spawning, or when they want to grow big quickly, off they go to the Great Feeding-Grounds.

It wasn't very long before Silver and the other smolts were thoroughly at home there, and the herrings and sand-eels had very little peace. It must have been about the middle of June when our smolts arrived at the Feeding-Grounds, and from then until the end of August they had a wonderful time, for the water was not too cold, and there was plenty of food everywhere. Through the whole of July and August the smolts just ate and grew, and ate and grew until they were almost big enough to be real salmon, and all the time Silver grew faster than any of the others. He grew so fast that if he had been separated from his companions for a few days and then had suddenly met them again, I doubt if they would have been able to recognise him!

But in September the water began to grow colder, and there was not quite such an abundance of food to be found. There was enough food all through the long, dark winter, but the tremendous feasting of July and August was over, and the salmon grew less quickly.

At the beginning of March, when winter still held the North in its grip (though perhaps a shade less firmly than of late), Silver began to feel restless once more. He was just two years old, and it would have been impossible to recognise the bright little smolt who had left the River-mouth less than a year ago. He was now a handsome bar of silver that weighed nearly ten pounds, and it was very hard to see any difference between him and a full-grown salmon, though he was still only what is called a "grilse." Up in the Feeding-Grounds were many of the others who had left the River at the same time as Silver, all of them beautiful fish, and one or two nearly as big as Silver himself. In some curious way, Silver's restlessness was connected with one of these others, a beautiful and graceful hen fish, and one day the restlessness made him start off with her towards the south. For days on end they travelled, slowly at first, then faster, past the mouths of many great salmon rivers, until at last they came to the mouth of the River they had left a few months before.

For a few days they lingered near the River-mouth, as though hating to leave the salt water, but it was not so pleasant as it had been. Silver felt heavy and irritable, and he no longer felt hungry when he saw the flash of a small fish in the water. And to make matters even worse, the Voice of the River was repeating over and over again ever so faintly but ever so clearly, "Come up and spawn, come up and spawn."

When they had been there a few days, the river current grew stronger and the water seemed fresher. And Silver's Lady (Grace was her name, for she was exactly that—divinely graceful) grew hourly more restless than Silver himself, until at last they started up the River together. As they went up, the current grew stronger and the water fresher and fresher, for there had been much rain up in the hills and the Great River was coming down in spate.

These two were not alone in their start for the Spawning-Beds. Large salmon, small salmon, other grilse like themselves, all were hurrying upstream to answer the call of the swollen River. It was one of those great years of the Salmon River, when rod-fishers and net-fishers both reap a rich harvest.

As they passed through each pool, some fish would stop to rest, but the River was still rising, and most of them kept on travelling up to the foot of the falls. If you had seen these falls, I daresay you would have wondered how any fish could possibly get over them. They were quite five feet high, and all the water of the Great River poured over them with a never-ceasing roar. But Silver and Grace had come to the River with a purpose, and Nature took care that she planted in them a determination strong enough to help them overcome all obstacles that lay between the River-mouth and the Spawning-Beds.

There were many salmon in the pool below the falls, small fish and large fish and huge fish, but every single one of them was quite determined to get over the falls and away to the good Spawning-Beds above. Silver and Grace lay there almost without moving for a day or two, resting quietly and gathering strength to be ready for the tremendous effort ahead of them. During each day they were quite still, but towards evening Silver would leave Grace, swim up to the surface of the slack water at the edge of the falls, and roll his back out of the water several times. It is difficult to say just why salmon have this habit, but it is nice to imagine that they are thinking about something, and do it for the same reason as we pace up and down a room when we are thinking particularly hard. If Silver was thinking about how to get over the falls (and very probably he was), his thoughts soon bore fruit. After a few rolls on the second evening, he swam back to Grace; then both of them swam right up under the falls and lay there on the bottom of the River. Quite suddenly Silver moved and swam in a slow circle. Two or three times he did this, then he swam as hard as he could straight up. When he came to the top he braced every muscle in his body, shot right out into the air, and hit the top of the falls with a splash. For a moment he hung there on the brink, struggling with all his might to swim upwards, then the current was too much for him and he was swept back into the pool. While he was resting on the bottom for another attempt, Grace did exactly as he had done, and came back again to rest beside him. Silver's next attempt was successful, and he swam over the top and on into the calm water of the next pool. In a very short while Grace was there too, and they lay together on the bottom, thankful to find still water and a quiet resting-place after such exhausting efforts.

While they were in this pool the River started to fall, and in a few days of fine weather it had dropped below its normal level. This caused our two grilse to remain in the pool, for the call of the River is naturally much less insistent when it is low than when it is high. Besides, it was a pleasant pool, and they had any amount of time in which to get up to the Spawning-Beds. But they were to learn that it is not possible to stay anywhere for very long without finding some exciting adventure.

For at least a week they lived quite happily in the pool, and they probably congratulated themselves many times on having found such a peaceful spot. I'm afraid they lived a lazy sort of life, for they did not feel inclined to eat, and indeed there was precious little in the River to feed a pair of hungry grilse even if they had felt so inclined. During most of the day they simply lay on the bottom of the pool, a short distance apart, and each behind a favourite rock. Once or twice during the day Silver would swim up and roll his back out of the water, and generally towards evening they would both play a little near the surface, and sometimes even jump right out into the air.

CHAPTER SIX

THE FIRST PERSON TO DISTURB THE PEACE OF THE POOL WHERE SILVER and Grace had settled down was that handsome gentleman in brown, the Otter. You will probably hear from lots of people that the otter never does much harm to salmon and trout; and a little later you'll probably be surprised because a lot of people will also tell you exactly the opposite. Actually it is not so very strange that there should be this difference of opinion; you must simply realise that both sides are right, and both are wrong! In other words, the truth, as usual, lies about half-way between the extreme ideas of the two sides. There are some otters in some rivers that do practically no harm to the salmon and trout. There are others that take salmon and trout quite often, and generally make a good meal off what they can catch. And there are others, again (I expect these are the strongest and best otters), that not only make a meal off all the finest salmon and trout they can catch when they are hungry, but sometimes bite and even kill salmon and trout just for the fun of it.

The otter that came to disturb Silver and Grace was one of this last kind. He was on his way upstream, a fine big fellow, able to swim almost as well as the swiftest and best of the salmon, and his little brain was fierce and quick and clever. Like the rest of us, he had to find food; and his size and speed gave him choice of all that was best. The first indication Silver and Grace had of his presence was a faint ripple on the surface of the pool, and then a glimpse of a dark brown shape coming down from above them with a trail of bubbles behind it. That faint ripple had warned them of danger, but they had not known what danger to expect. Their brains, well trained in the ways of Nature, flashed a swift message to their muscles, and before the otter was two feet below the surface of the water Silver and Grace had started away for safety. But for all their speed and strength, they were not to escape quite unharmed. Either Grace was not quite quick enough, or else the otter had picked her and not Silver as likely to make him a good meal. Almost before she was well started, the brown gentleman's teeth had snapped, and blood was flowing from a gash near her tail. But that was all; the sharp teeth had failed to grip, and the pain from her wound drove Grace upstream at a pace which gave the otter no hope of catching her. Actually he turned quickly to follow her, and as he did so, another salmon, too frightened to know what was happening, darted across in front of him. The powerful jaws opened and closed again; this time they found a grip, and the otter swam to the surface struggling with his catch.

Our two grilse were so disturbed by this adventure that they travelled upstream through several pools before they dared to rest again. Grace was very impatient. The wound from the otter's teeth was a bad one, and

instinct warned her that she must get to the Spawning-Beds as quickly as possible. Already the blood-sucking fresh-water parasites had fastened themselves to the raw edges of the wound, and often she would jump out of the water again and again in despairing efforts to shake off the irritating pests.

But they did break their journey once more, at the pool just below the place where the Little Stream runs into the Great Salmon River, and here it was that Silver met with yet another adventure. One day he was lying on the bottom of the River, close beside Grace, and they were both motionless save for the faintest fanning movement of their broad tails. Gradually Silver began to notice a little shrimp-like thing that kept darting about just under the surface of the water, and almost directly above where he lay. It disappeared, only to turn up again a minute or two later. Silver began to grow annoyed. Was *he*, one of the lords of the River, one of the knights in shining armour—was he to suffer annoyance from a little shrimp-like thing less than an inch long? Certainly not; and with a swirl of his tail he shot towards the surface of the water and seized the offending object in his powerful jaws. Satisfied, he turned down towards the bottom again. There was a sharp jerk, a sudden pain in his jaw—and he remembered. This little shrimp of a thing was stronger than him, just as a mysterious little olive dun had been stronger than when he was a parr.

But all that did not occur to him at once. When he felt the pain and the jerk he just shook his head and turned again to go down to the bottom of the pool, probably with the idea of thinking things out for a minute or two.

The little shrimp-like thing had other ideas. It was pulling and straining at him, giving him no chance to think or get down among the rocks. All at once he was terrified, and he darted off in a mad rush downstream to the tail of the pool. He stopped there, but the thing was still holding him, jerking and pulling, giving him no rest at all. Furiously he rushed back again, and savagely he shook his head as he came out of the water in two glorious leaps at the end of his rush. Still the hook was in his jaw, and now it seemed to be coaxing him ever so gently towards the bank. He allowed himself to be coaxed, seeking to regain his scattered wits. Something moved close beside him in the water, and away he dashed again. Several times the same thing happened, until he began to grow tired, and at last he had no strength to make another run. He lay quietly on his side while he was drawn over the net, and he allowed himself to be lifted on to the bank without a single kick.

By rights that should be the end of this story, but as a matter of fact it isn't at all. Silver was in luck once more, for it was the Good Fisherman who had landed him, and the Good Fisherman was not slow to recognise the mark on that silly little fin near Silver's tail. He read the number on the disc and laughed quietly. "So you're back again, my giant parr," he said. "You're a fine big grilse, but I trust you to grow into something bigger than this before I see you again. A parr as big as you were should make a Sixty-pounder some day."

All the time he was talking his fingers were working quickly to get the fly out of Silver's mouth. The second it was out he slipped Silver back into the water, held him there a moment and then watched him swim slowly away.

Silver went straight back to deep water and lay there beside Grace, rather ashamed of himself. If he thought about it at all, he must have been mystified by the whole business. Twice he had been dragged about the River by a tiny little thing that seemed untiring, twice he had been lifted out on to the bank and twice returned to the River. You and I can see the reason easily enough, for we know that the Good Fisherman was a great sportsman, that he had marked Silver when he caught him as a parr, and that he hoped and expected that Silver would grow into a gigantic salmon one day. But Silver knew nothing of all this. He probably thought that he had escaped from danger by his own skill, just as he had escaped from the otter.

Whatever he thought about it, the adventure had one useful result. He understood at last why it was that Grace was in such a hurry to get to the Spawning-Beds, for he felt battered and bruised after his long fight. And as he lay on the bottom something inside him said, "Hurry, before your strength is all gone." That night the two fish turned out of the Great Salmon River up the Little Stream towards the Spawning-Beds.

CHAPTER SEVEN

THERE IS NOTHING THAT DRIVES A SALMON TO SUCH TERRIFIC EFFORTS as the fear that exhaustion will overcome him before he can spawn. Silver and Grace were both driven on by this fear. The exertion of ascending the River coupled with their long fast (for all practical purposes they had eaten nothing since leaving the salt water) would have weakened them in any case. But, besides this natural drain on their vitality, a very great deal of Grace's strength was being sapped by the parasites that clung to her wound, and Silver had expended much energy in his fight to avoid capture by the Good Fisherman. And so, from the time they entered the Little Stream, their thoughts were only of when and how and where to spawn.

Grace was very fussy and particular, as all good mothers are. She must have this and she must have that: nice clean gravel, a run of bright fresh water, not too deep and not too shallow, yet sheltered from the main force of the stream in flood-time. The eggs must be well cared for by the stream, or it was not worth laying them at all! And in the end she picked exactly the same spot as Silver's father and mother had chosen. Even then she grumbled a bit about "there being too much water after heavy rain," but on the whole she seemed pretty well satisfied.

Being satisfied, she was more peaceful; and Silver was no longer in a hurry, so for several days they lay side by side near the chosen spot. They were very different fish from the two beautiful creatures that had left the salt water. Their silver jackets were rusty and dull, their firm, graceful bodies were thin and flabby, and their heads seemed to have grown larger than of old. And every day they were more nearly ready to spawn, until at last Grace began to lay her first eggs.

Probably you have seen salmon spawning by this time, but if you have not, and if you live near a Salmon River, you should go see them, for it is one of the most interesting sights in the world. Grace was lying on the chosen gravel. At first she lay quite still, then she began to fan furiously with her tail, and suddenly she was still again. Many times she repeated these movements, and every now and then she would turn on her side as though to scrape her scales on the gravel. Close behind her was Silver, and there were three long scars on his side to show that he had had to fight other cock salmon to assert his right to Grace. He did his share of the work more quickly, but every now and then he would turn to chase the small trout that hung around to gobble up the eggs, or another cock salmon who dared approach too close to Grace.

Even when they had done spawning the two fish stayed close to the beds for a few days longer, as though to watch over the eggs. Grace by this time had grown very weak, and the parasites that clung to her wound troubled her more and more, but Silver was quite strong for a spent salmon. Of course he was far from being a perfectly healthy fish, but he had come through the ordeal of spawning quite as well as any salmon ever does, and very soon he was anxious to get back to the salt water. Grace started with him when he turned downstream, but her weakness made her very slow, and I am sorry to say that before long Silver had left her, and was well on his way down the River alone. Nature's children never wait for anything that is weak and feeble. It is one of the rules of existence that they learn from the start, and Silver was ever a faithful follower of Nature's rules. Very probably he knew that Grace was not strong enough to reach the salt water again, for in less than two days after he had left her she found that she could no longer keep upright in the water. A few days more she lingered on, growing weaker and weaker, lying on her side gasping for breath on the bottom of a pool, until at last she quivered and lay still. Her job was done, and she had paid the penalty that Nature exacts for one single second's slowness in the face of danger.

I'm afraid it's not very likely that Silver thought a great deal about Grace on his way down to the sea. At first he may have missed her companionship a little, but he was on his way to the sea once more, and every day that passed brought him nearer to it, and gave him so much joy and hope that there was no time to think of the things of the past. Back to the sea: back to the salt water that went to his head like champagne, back to chase sand-eels and herrings, to regain health and strength and a purple silver sheen on his scales.

It was a slow journey, for he was much exhausted and could do little more than drift downstream in easy stages. December had come by the time he reached the mouth of the River, and he was nearly three years old, a long, thin, rather sad-looking grilse kelt. Even then he was not ready for the long journey to the Great Feeding-Grounds, and he spent many days near the River-mouth feeding on sand-eels, renewing the silver of his scales and regaining his strength. There were a few other kelts at the River-mouth, all bent on recovering condition, but Silver and Grace had spawned early, and so Silver was among the very first to start on the great northward journey.

Of that journey itself there is not a great deal to be told. The kelts chased every herring school they saw, and feasted upon everything they could find. They met with few adventures and much food; and Silver wasted a good deal of time in wondering why he had ever left the salt water. When he reached the cold waters to the north of Iceland, he swore that there was no place in the world like the sea, and I wouldn't be surprised to hear that he told himself that he would never go back to the River again. In any case, he soon settled down at the Great Feeding-Grounds, as though he intended to stay there for ever, and it was two whole years before he felt the restlessness of the spawning urge again; every single day of that time he spent in feasting and growing and learning new lessons.

It is not very easy to tell of the adventures he met with during those years, for no one knows very much of the Great Feeding-Grounds. But perhaps we can make pretty good guesses about a few of them. The Great Feeding-Grounds are never free from exciting incidents, for there are very many beasts and fish there, and death is on every side, as it always is in the sea. Small things make food for little fish, big fish feed on little fish, and bigger fish feed on the big fish, and so on until you come to the whales, and these when they die make food for every fish that swims. But there was much for Silver to feed on, and he grew rapidly into a glorious salmon, strong and beautiful and speedy as the most perfect athlete; and consequently he was well able to avoid his innumerable enemies.

Nearly every day of a salmon's life in the Great Feeding-Grounds is spent in pursuit of the herring shoals. One day Silver and a number of the other salmon found a particularly large shoal of herring, and (being hungry, as usual) they set to work as though there was a law that they must eat quickly or not at all. There were thousands upon thousands of herrings in the shoal, all massed together, and Silver made rush after rush right into the middle of them. He was so full that he was almost bursting, and he had just begun to form an idea that it might be a good thing to lie on the bottom somewhere until he felt hungry again, when he saw a dark shape in the water behind him. An otter, he thought, as he dived for safety, but he was wrong. There were several dark shapes, and they were porpoises. Salmon darted in every direction, jumped right out of the water, swam scuttering along the top of the water, but all to no purpose: they were heavy and slow with over-feeding, and the porpoises caught them one after another, all save Silver and a few wise ones who headed for deep water at the very first warning of danger.

That was Silver's first experience of porpoises, but not by any means his last. And very soon too he learned a little about the seals whose shiny heads sometimes dot the whole surface of the Great Feeding-Grounds till the sea looks like a wide expanse of green spotted dog pudding. A seal loves to swim suddenly under a school of salmon, catch one amid the confusion that follows, and then swim to the surface to play with the poor fish as a cat plays with a mouse until it is dead. You will see him throw a salmon into the air and catch it as it comes down, let it go for a moment, then dive and catch it again, and shake it as a terrier shakes a rat. But Silver had no intention of making a meal for one of these gentlemen, and so he and a few others would leave the school and go off alone when a seal appeared; for they knew that a seal prefers to make his rush into the middle of a mass of fish, just as a salmon picks the thickest part of a herring shoal for his rush, or as a bad shot aims at the middle of a covey of partridges!

So passed two whole years, and Silver began to feel restless again. By this time he was a magnificent salmon, shapely and altogether beautiful,

and he weighed just over thirty pounds. But the most remarkable thing about him was that he was destined to become one of those very rare salmon who return to their rivers to spawn more than twice. So far he had only spawned once, but the restlessness grew and grew inside him until he started again towards the south.

It was an uneventful journey as far as the north of Scotland, though he had one unpleasantly narrow escape from a hungry shark. Some three days after he first reached Scotland came what was probably the narrowest escape from death that Silver ever had in his life. He was swimming steadily along a few yards behind several other salmon when suddenly the leader seemed to strike an invisible wall. Several of the others also came to a sudden stop and began struggling furiously, and Silver saw that they were entangled in what looked like a spider's web. He was almost on top of it himself, and had no time to turn, so he leaped high out of the water in sheer panic. And this was the only thing that saved his life, for he jumped clear over the line of corks that supported the net, and found himself swimming freely away on the other side. He came up against a good many nets after that, and as he was never caught in a sea net, I rather fancy that he had learned the lesson of this experience, and made a regular habit of leaping over the corks.

When he eventually arrived safe and sound at the mouth of the Great Salmon River Silver found many other salmon, all there on the same errand as himself. Everything was very much as it had always been at the River-mouth, yet there was a difference. Silver was now a real salmon, as big as almost any other fish, and handsomer than the best of them. By reason of this, he found no difficulty in selecting a very beautiful hen-fish of about twenty-four pounds as his wife. The two of them made a magnificent couple, and they are an excellent example of one of Nature's wisest laws. Among wild things you will always find that the biggest and handsomest males secure the best wives. You may think that this is just an accident, but Nature is far too wise to let her domain be controlled by accident. That clever old lady is always planning and scheming to improve her children and to increase her stock of them. She says to herself, "Handsome, healthy parents mean handsomer, healthier children, and more of 'em," and so she takes jolly good care to bring the handsome couples together, just as she generally prevents deformed or weak and sickly things from having any children at all. Her school is a hard one, but it breeds the right sort, and we human beings can learn a great deal from her methods if we will.

But in singing the praises of Dame Nature I have forgotten all about Silver and his new-found wife. These two felt far too happy to leave the salt water at once, and they spent several weeks near the River-mouth waiting for rain in the hills to strengthen the Voice of the fresh water calling them upstream to the Spawning-Beds.

Probably they passed most of this waiting in chasing the sand-eels, and I daresay they enjoyed being together. Silver probably showed his lady how high he could jump out of the water and how fast he could swim. And she probably watched and admired, and sometimes jumped out of the water or swam nearly as fast as he did, just to show that she could. These modern girls who can play tennis and golf so well are not really so vastly different from the old order of things.

CHAPTER EIGHT

ALL GOOD THINGS COME TO AN END SOONER OR LATER, OTHERWISE Nature's business would never go forward at all. Silver and his Lady soon found that their appetites were growing less keen, and they noticed that the fresh-water currents from the River were becoming stronger and darker in colour, until before long the old song was calling to them: "Come up and spawn, come up and spawn." Millions of salmon have heard that call, and millions will hear it again, but there never has been and never will be a salmon who failed to do everything in his power to answer it. Once the call has been heard, death is the only obstacle that can block the way to the Spawning-Beds with any hope of success.

So Silver and his new Grace left their beloved sea once more, though many salmon had not yet heard the call and still played around the River-mouth dreaming about the halcyon days at the Feeding-Grounds, and perhaps of the dangers that lay ahead of them on their way up the River.

Our salmon travelled easily at first, for the call of the River was still gentle, begging rather than commanding them to ascend it, soothing them on their way rather than driving them to a frenzy of eagerness. But its very gentleness was compelling, and they did not break their journey until they came to the pool at the foot of the falls. Here Silver found a great change, and it was some while before he could make it out at all. On the right-hand side of the fall there seemed to be a new little stream with a smooth white bed and smooth white banks, and made up of a series of little falls that offered no difficulty of ascent to a salmon. Actually it was what is known as a fish ladder; a number of concrete steps making several little falls out of a big one, designed to help the salmon to get over the falls and so to the Spawning-Beds. Once he had grasped the flow of new currents in the pool, Silver was not much interested. He had proved his ability to get over the falls when he was a grilse, and now that he was a magnificent thirty-pounder he was quite sure he could surmount any obstacle. As a matter of fact he was a wee bit swollen-headed. He knew quite well that there were not a great many salmon bigger than himself, and he knew that the salmon were lords of the River; like many people who are great and important, he had an idea that he was just a bit greater and more important than he really was.

They had not been many days in the pool before Silver learned that however big a salmon may be, those mysterious beings on the bank are disrespectful enough to give him very little peace. All day long there were fishermen at the pool: gaudy flies, flashing minnows and irritating red prawns tempted them to rashness from dawn till dark. Silver had learned his lesson as a grilse, and had no intention of touching any of the lures, though he often followed them across the pool, and was never quite sure of himself when a be-whiskered red prawn hovered tantalisingly in front of his nose. His Lady was very rash indeed. Again and again Silver had his work cut out to restrain her from seizing one of these dainty things that danced so gracefully in the river current. Twice he had to shoulder her away from a curious little prawn that swung across the River several feet in front of where they were lying.

Just why she was so anxious to seize these things, and why Silver himself was so sorely tempted at times, is hard to say. Certainly neither of them knew why it was, for they did not feel hunger at all. Perhaps there are a good many reasons, all of them rather small ones, and all pretty much the same in the end. When a salmon is on his way up the river to spawn he has no need of food—indeed, his stomach is not able to digest food at all, and even if it were able to, there would not be enough food in the rivers to satisfy one-tenth of all the salmon that go up to spawn. Perhaps he finds the angler's lures very like the food that he works so hard to catch in the sea, and the sight of this food hovering almost in his jaws is too tempting to be resisted. And it is worth remembering that a big salmon on his way to spawn has a temper rather like that of an old Colonel who has missed his breakfast to catch a train and be in time for an important appointment, then missed the train as well! Very likely, too, he sometimes thinks that the little shiny Devon minnow is darting across to take some of his lady's eggs.

Whatever are the rights and wrongs of it all, it is a question that has puzzled anglers for years and years. Sometimes it turns them from peace-loving gentlemen into pugnacious pen-pushers, as irritable as the King of old cock salmon himself. And that, again, is simply because they will not see that both sides are partly right. A salmon need not eat anything while he is in fresh water, but while in the salt water he has formed a habit of darting at a flash, and finding that, when he catches it, the flash is good to eat. This habit cannot be shaken off entirely, and so in fresh water the salmon does occasionally seize something, and perhaps even swallow it.

But this has taken us far from the fortunes of Silver and his Lady.

While we were worrying about all this, they left the Falls Pool and travelled on upstream to a pool that was less disturbed by fishermen. Almost as soon as they got there the River began to drop. Day after day the sun shone, and there was no rain in the hills; the water grew warmer and less full of oxygen. Silver was putting on his spawning uniform, and as his bright sides turned rusty and dull, his temper was shorter and more uncertain than ever. If any fisherman had come along to the pool and dangled a nice little prawn in front of his nose just then, I'm pretty sure it would have been the end of things. Fortunately none came, but Silver's bad temper led him to do one thing so curious that I would not dare to write of it had I not seen it happen with my own eyes.

This is how it happened. Not far from the pool two smart little black-and-white wagtails had a nest, and every day they would hunt along the edge of the pool to find flies and other food. They used to strut about close to the water's edge, searching each weed-covered rock that the falling River had left high and dry. One day, when Silver must have been feeling even more irritable than usual, he saw one of the little birds bobbing about just above him. You know how a wagtail works at the edge of the water: a few quick, sharp little steps, a flutter into the air, back again, more little strutting steps, and always a long, slim tail balancing him and beating time, as though to keep him in step. On this particular day the wagtail searched for a long time just above the place where Silver lay close under the bank. This must have got on the old fellow's nerves, for he made a sudden rush to the top of the water and grabbed at the bird with his fierce jaws. Fortunately the wagtail was too quick, but it must have been an unpleasant shock, because the two little birds always kept some distance from the water after that day.

The rest of that summer was a dull time for our two fish. The River scarcely rose an inch for weeks, so they stayed in the same pool until the autumn rains freshened the water and the swollen currents urged them to

hurry on to the Spawning-Beds. There is little to be told of the journey up to Silver's favourite place in the Little Stream or of the actual spawning, but one more adventure fell to Silver's lot as he lay watching the eggs and gathering his strength to return to the sea. He was caught in a net for the first and last time in his life.

Salmon, for all their dignity and nobility and strength, are not very good at taking care of themselves, particularly when they first hatch from their eggs. Men have learnt this, and since they want as many as possible of the baby salmon to grow into thirty- or forty-pounders, they try to protect the young fish as much as they can. With this idea, they sometimes net the fish that are ready to spawn, strip them of their eggs, then hatch the eggs in boxes with water flowing through them and rear the little salmon until they are almost ready to go down to the sea.

It happened that the men came to the Little Stream to net spawning salmon for this purpose while Silver was still there. The first thing he knew about it was a splashing upstream which came closer and closer, until at last he turned and rushed down with several other fish, straight into a net. The net was hauled on to the bank, and several men started to untangle the fish. One of them said: "Four hen fish and a cock."

"Yes," answered another; "but the cock is no good. He's spawned already."

Someone picked Silver very gently out of the net and slipped him back into the water; but the Good Fisherman was there, and he had seen the little disc that he had clipped on to Silver's adipose fin. That is how we know about this adventure.

Silver was very weak when he got back into the water, far weaker than his Lady, who had somehow escaped the stripper's net. Cock fish always seem to feel the effort of spawning more than hen fish do—so much so that very few of them recover after spawning once. Silver would very probably have died on this occasion had not his Lady been so anxious to get back to the sea. As it was they both started off downstream almost as soon as the men had left the Little Stream that evening, though Silver was able to do very little more than keep himself drifting down with the current. He was careful to guard what strength he had left by resting frequently, and always behind a big rock or some other good shelter from the force of the stream, and at long last he got back to the River-mouth. Even here his strength only returned very slowly; but it did return, and eventually he was ready for another journey to the Great Feeding-Grounds.

CHAPTER NINE

IT WOULD BE QUITE EASY TO MAKE UP ALL KINDS OF AMUSING STORIES about Silver's return to the Great Feeding-Grounds, and about his life there; and it is very likely that any imaginary stories we could make up would be far less extraordinary than what actually happened. Silver was an exceptional fish (that is why this story is written about him). He returned to the River to spawn more often than do the vast majority of salmon, and consequently he met with more adventures than most salmon. But it would be a pity to make him seem impossible by inventing stories about him when there are so many true ones waiting to be told.

That is why we'll pass over this journey of Silver's to the Feeding-Grounds, and simply say that he arrived safely, and stayed there two more years. He found the same old joy in the glorious freedom of the salt water, in the wildness of the waves on stormy days and nights, in the chase of the herring schools and in the return of his health and strength. He fed mightily while he was in the north upon everything he could catch. And he grew so much that he weighed over fifty pounds when he returned to the River once more—one of the finest and biggest fish that had ever run up to spawn.

Silver's size and strength made him very proud, and a good deal more careless than he had been in his young days. He found his old mate at the River-mouth (she was now a beautiful thirty-pounder with many black spots on her silver sides to tell of her former visit to the River), and together they ran up to the Falls Pool. It was here that Silver showed the first signs of his new recklessness. A gaudy salmon fly danced across the pool, and Silver snapped at it at once. Fortunately he missed and it flicked away. Something or other (it may have been the memory of his previous experience of gaudy flies, or a glimpse of the fisherman on the bank) warned him not to try again, and though the same fly and many different ones came dancing above its head during the next few hours, he did not move again.

They lingered in the pool for some days, but the same old trouble came again. More than one fisherman had seen Silver's mighty back and shoulders rolling out of the water, and each fisherman who saw it swore a mighty oath that he'd catch this monster. So they tried all day and every day with large flies and small flies, dark flies and bright flies, but not once did Silver or his Lady make a move to encourage them. Then rain fell in the hills, the water freshened and away went the salmon, over the falls and up the River. Silver felt strong and determined, and his temper was very uncertain. By the time they had reached the next rest pool he felt that he could fight anything, and all knowledge of fear had slipped back into the recesses of his brain. The freshness of the water from the hills had gone to his head like wine, and he longed to test himself, to learn if the joy and strength he felt in his heart were really there or not. And that must have been why he made a terrific rush at the first fly that came over him after they got to the rest pool.

Nature evidently intended that he should learn a lesson this time. Written in golden letters, and before all other things, you will find in her book of commandments to wild creatures: "Thou shalt not lose thy fear of danger." Silver had lost all his fear when he seized the fly, but he found it again a moment later. There was the same old jerk as the fisherman struck to drive the hook home, and the well-remembered strain of the rod attempting to draw him into the bank. Silver ran upstream like a mad thing, then turned and came down again in a still more furious rush. The man on the bank followed as best he could, and gasped with amazement and delight when he saw the fish for a moment and realised his size. But the fight was only just begun, for the man on the bank was not the Good Fisherman. Silver soon found that there was very little strain on his mouth, and he was able to do much as he liked, running like a torpedo-boat, jumping out of the water, turning and twisting every way to loosen the hook. But it was well and truly fixed in his jaw, and all his efforts were unavailing till he remembered the advice of an old salmon: "It's the big rocks on the bottom that are your best friends. They shelter you from the current, they hide you, they help you when the fishermen hook you. When all else fails, go to them."

All else had failed, and the rocks would have failed Silver too if the fisherman had been worth his salt. As it was, the great fish sank like a stone to the River-bed, close behind a big rock. The fisherman let him go, glad of respite for himself—he did not know the salmon-fisher's golden rule: "Never give your fish a single second's peace." Long before he woke up again, Silver was settled in position, head on the bottom, tail pointing straight up. Fishermen say that a salmon is "sulking" when he is in this position, and he cannot be moved by the strain of the rod. As Silver lay there the gut was up against the sharp edge of his chosen rock, and he began to work his head from side to side, fraying the gut against the roughness of the rock. The fisherman felt the vibration of this movement, and he put on all the strain he dared. It was too late. Suddenly the frayed gut snapped, and Silver was free once more, with a fly in his mouth and half a yard of heavy gut trailing from it. And the fisherman? He just walked sadly back to the lodge and told his tale of the lost monster to an audience that laughed unsympathetically—and it served him right. There's no salmon in this world that can sulk if a fisherman knows his job and keeps him bothered all the time.

It was not long before our two salmon had to move again. Other eyes than those of the angler who had hooked him soon spotted Silver's great back rolling out of the water on the calm, still evenings. All who saw that back swore that he must weigh fifty pounds, and some talked of sixty or even seventy pounds, for most anglers over-estimate the weight of a big salmon when they see him in the water. So they all did their best to catch him, and they bothered the pool just as much as they had bothered the Falls Pool, until Silver and his Lady moved on.

Silver found a new delight in the River as they travelled up to the Spawning-Beds. Usually the sea holds all that brings delight and happiness and well-being to a salmon. Silver was no less fond of the sea than the rest of his kind, but whereas they seldom return more than once, or twice at the most, to spawn, this was already Silver's third visit. He had had so many adventures in the River that every bend of it, every rock and every cross current seemed to recall some memory, even if it was only vaguely remembered from the time of his first return as a grilse. It was pleasant to see some of the wild creatures of the River-bank, and even the trout and pike seemed less contemptible than of old. Nearly all of them re-membered him, and hastened to show their admiration for his magnificent size and his handsome shape. The little dipper who had bobbed up and down the edge of the Bridge Pool for years, and whose nest was always under the same arch of the bridge, was simply amazed. "What a fine great fish ye are, my lord!" she said, and added that she minded the time when he was no bigger than a trout, "but ever so much more handsome, of course!" And the huge twenty-five-pound pike whose lair was under the shelf of the right bank of the Hut Pool snapped all his thousand teeth at the sight of a salmon more than twice as big as himself.

As for Alderman Speckles, the ten-pound trout who lived in the Railway Pool, he said privately to his wife, "Well, my dear, I think there must be somethng in this going-down-to-the-sea business, after all. Have you seen what it has done for young Silver?" That, from a trout, is very high praise, for trout do know quite well that they miss something by not going down to the sea, although, like most human beings under similar circumstances, they would rather pretend that they are better off as they are.

The rest of the journey to the Little Stream was simply a dignified and stately triumphal progress. Silver was Lord of the whole River at last, and he knew it, and made the most of it. They arrived at the beds in good time for the spawning, and settled themselves to wait quietly and grandly till all was ready: then came the rude awakening that always comes when people are most pleased with themselves.

Normally there are very few poachers along the banks of Silver's River, but in this particular year there were a great many unemployed men in the district. You probably know something of what this means from hearing grown-ups talk, and later on you'll know a great deal more about it—at least I hope you will, because there is very little hope of better things until all the young people of Britain buckle down to learn something about this terrible problem. But that is beside the point just now. I must tell you how unemployment very nearly closed Silver's life-story.

In a small town not far from the Spawning-Beds there were a good many pretty hard characters, and most of them were out of a job. Some of these men (they were not bad men; poachers seldom are, for if things were slightly different they'd mostly be sportsmen) were finding that winter a difficult time to get enough food, and so they decided to do a little poaching. One night, as Silver and his Lady lay resting near the beds, they saw a light shining on the water. The two fish did not pay much attention at first, but as the light drew closer and became brighter and more fascinating they were interested, and swam closer to investigate. Then they became so fascinated that they could do nothing but gaze and gaze straight at the light, and of course they could see nothing of the dark figures on the bank behind it. One of the men whispered, "Get the big 'un, Bill." There was a splash as something hit the water, and Silver felt a burning pain in his side.

The man with the spear had made a bad shot, and only hit Silver a glancing blow. Silver rushed away to hide under the bank, and his Lady came with him. But the light still shone, and she could not resist its fascination. She turned and swam back to it; there was another splash, and she was lifted out of the water struggling and fighting on to the bank.

The light moved off downstream, and Silver was never bothered with it again. A few days later he found a new mate, and before long they were ready to spawn. On the day that the female dropped her first eggs the Good Fisherman came along the stream to look for spawning fish. He crept slowly up to the bank of the stream near where Silver lay, and looked over the edge of the bank. He saw Silver and his mate lying there, and gasped with delight. It was a sight to make any fisherman gasp. Two huge salmon lying side by side in the clear shallow water, the male a good fifty pounds, and the female perhaps ten pounds less. They lay there with their great tails gently moving, and the Good Fisherman could see everything: the fly that was still firmly fixed in Silver's jaw, the gash from the poacher's spear, even the aluminium mark on the fin near his tail.

The Good Fisherman cursed softly. "Unless I'm mistaken," he said to himself, "that's the fish I marked more than seven years ago. That's Jim's fly in his mouth, and the poachers made that wound in his side. I always knew he'd grow to a big 'un, and I hoped I'd catch him weighing sixty pounds some day. I'll never do it now. That gash will kill him long before he feels salt water again."

CHAPTER TEN

"THAT GASH WILL KILL HIM BEFORE HE FEELS SALT WATER AGAIN." THE
Good Fisherman was very nearly right. Almost any other salmon but Silver
would have died from the effects of such a wound at spawning time, but
Silver, for a number of reasons, was the exception to some of the rules
that govern the habits and powers of the salmon family. He was always
an abnormally healthy fish, because he had never experienced any difficulty about getting good food and plenty of it, because he was born of
good healthy parents, and because he had gone to the sea when he was
only one year old. And it is very probable that his powers of recovery
were greater than those of most salmon, because he had returned oftener
to fresh water and consequently had developed these powers.

In any case, the Good Fisherman was wrong in the end, though it seemed for a long time that he would be right. When Silver felt the healing salt water surrounding his body once more he was a very sick fish indeed. His progress down the River from the Spawning-Beds had been slow and painful, he had lost condition terribly, though he was still far from being as thin and lanky as most kelts; and parasites by the score had attached themselves to his wound. The sand-eels at the River-mouth soon did a great deal towards restoring his full strength, and the parasites did not flourish on a healthy-skinned, active fish in the salt water as they had flourished on the sluggish, feeble Silver who had drifted down the River. And Silver's usual luck did not desert him, for he came across a shoal of herrings bound in the same direction as himself almost as soon as he was able to follow them. For days he travelled with them, taking a heavy toll and sorely taxing his unpractised stomach. Long before they reached the Feeding-Grounds he felt himself as good as the great fifty-pounder who had travelled down from the north a year or so before.

At the Feeding-Grounds Silver wrought terrible havoc among the herring schools, until he was just as strong as he had ever been, and a little bit bigger than he had ever been. About that time he came upon a school of herrings that were larger than usual and a little more pleasant to swallow. This school was heading in a westerly direction when Silver found them, and he followed them, passing between Greenland and the land that lies round the North Pole, right on beyond Baffin Land and Bank's Land until they were almost due north of the mighty Mackenzie River that comes down all through the frozen Yukon district of Canada from the Great Slave Lake. And somewhere about there they came upon the Feeding-Grounds of the huge Tyee Salmon of British Columbia.

Silver had seen many strange things as he followed the herring school, but nothing amazed him so much as the discovery of these huge salmon that were almost exactly like himself. By this time he weighed quite fifty-five pounds, but among the Tyees he seemed almost small. There were very few fish of less than thirty pounds to be seen, and some weighed well over a hundred pounds—a few must have been a hundred and twenty pounds. They were very much like Silver to look at, but a little deeper and shorter in proportion to their weight, and not quite so bright.

Before long Silver made friends with one of them, a huge gruff old fellow weighing about ninety pounds, and from him he learned many strange things. One of Silver's first questions was about the small salmon. He wanted to know if all Tyees were born weighing thirty pounds. Old Chinook (that was the name of the ninety-pound Tyee) laughed a good bit to himself at that question, but he was courteous, as salmon always are, and explained it as carefully as he could. In a way Silver was right, but really he was quite wrong. There is no such thing as a Tyee weighing less than thirty pounds. When a Tyee first goes to the sea from the River he is not called a Tyee at all, but only a Quinnat or Spring Salmon. The fish that weigh over thirty pounds are generally together in schools, and most of the younger ones stay in their own schools until they grown large enough to join the others.

Old Chinook was a fish from the famous Campbell River on Vancouver Island, and he had wonderful tales to tell of the hundreds of boats that lie off the River-mouth in August and September to try to catch the Tyees, and of all the thousands of other boats belonging to the professional fishermen. He said that it was almost impossible to be out of hearing of a motor-boat engine all the way from Alaska to Vancouver, and even south of there to the Sacramento River and San Francisco and Monterey Bay in California.

He showed Silver a great fish of a hundred and thirty pounds, who belonged to the Nimpkish River, and was said to be the largest fish at the Feeding-Grounds. In return Silver told him many of his own adventures, but Old Chinook found them hard to believe. "You say you've been back to spawn three times already?" he asked. Silver insisted that he had. "Well," said Old Chinook, "there's five different kinds of salmon that go every year to the rivers of Western Canada, and I guess there's millions and millions of each kind, but I never yet heard of more than an odd one or two that got back from the trip once, let alone three times!"

That is perfectly true. If you go to the Rivers of Western Canada some time between October and January (and if you are lucky you will go there one day), you can see all the different salmon—the Sockeyes, the Humpies, the Dogs, the Cohos and the Tyees—spawning in their thousands. And when the spawning is over you can see them in thousands dead and dying along the banks and on the beds of the rivers. It sounds as though Nature is terribly wasteful, but she has good reasons. She found that she had to send thousands and thousands of salmon up the rivers every winter so that the seals and otters and porpoises, the blackfish and eagles and mink and coon might eat their fill during the long winter, and she must have decided that if she let each one of them come back and spawn two or three times there would be no room at all in the rivers.

Now that the white man has come to Western Canada, with his cunning nets and his boats with engines, all the different salmon runs are growing smaller. Perhaps the Dog salmon run is almost as big as ever, but there are so many of these fish that nothing ever could affect their numbers noticeably. The Cohos and Sockeyes and Tyees grow fewer and fewer every year. One day Nature will begin to be afraid that they will die out altogether, and then perhaps she'll let them go back to the sea after they have spawned and run up the Rivers a second time. I wonder?

But if it tried to record all the tales that Silver and Chinook exchanged, this book would never end. In between story-telling times the two old fellows simply gorged on the herrings of the Beaufort Sea and the Arctic Ocean, for these were very good and very plentiful. One day, with two or three other Tyees, they chased a school right up to the place

81

where the sea ends and the ice begins. Just as the first of the Tyees reached the ice there was a splash, a flash of white in the water, and he disappeared. Silver still knew danger when he saw it, and he glided away as quickly as he could, a little puzzled, because he had never before seen danger of that kind in the Feeding-Grounds. It reminded him of the death of his last mate.

Old Chinook knew all about it, though. He told Silver that it was a Polar Bear, and he went on to describe the speed with which bears can hook a fish out of the water. That, of course, led to an endless series of stories about the black bears on the Vancouver Island rivers, who divide their time between dabbing at salmon with their great forepaws and eating berries.

But the time soon came for Silver to leave Old Chinook and turn back towards the east and the Feeding-Grounds of the Atlantic Salmon. He had grown very rapidly during his stay among the Tyees, and by this time he weighed a good sixty pounds. He felt very strong and fearless, and was quite determined to stay in the sea for ever. But something had drawn him back to his own Feeding-Grounds, and it was still bothering him and drawing him on still further. Suddenly he recognised the call, "Come up and spawn; come up and spawn." Very faint it was, but quite relentless, and it had to be answered. Before long he was on his way south for the last time, lazily swimming towards the Great Salmon River.

He met with all the usual adventures by the way. Twice he was careless enough to get entangled in the nets, and in one or two of the cottages of the North Scottish fisher folk you may still hear the tale of the mighty fish that got into the net one night and just tore it to ribbons to get out again. Near the River-mouth he almost lost his life to the old seal who lived on the island there, and as it was he lost a big piece out of his shoulder through being too slow.

This wound made him careful of seals, but in other ways he was

terribly careless. He was a glorious fish, deep and wide, shining silver and very strong, and he knew it. He was bigger than any other fish at the River-mouth, always irritable and very impatient. The River was very low, but he felt the call to go up very strong within him, and that was why he ran right through the Falls Pool with the first small freshet that came.

CHAPTER ELEVEN

SOMETIMES I WONDER WHAT WOULD HAVE BEEN THE END OF SILVER had it not been for that piece bitten out of his shoulder by the old black seal, and for the hot, dry weather of the year when it happened. The wound in his shoulder was driving him almost frantic, for it warned him continually that unless he hurried he would never get to the Spawning-Beds in time; and all the while the urge to get there was far stronger within him than it had ever been before. That was why he rushed up to the Falls Pool on the first sign of a rise in the River, though he knew quite well there would be no more rain in the hills for many days to come. That was why he kept jumping in mad, vain attempts to get over the falls, though he knew the River was too low for it to be possible for any salmon to get over them, and that it was dropping lower every day.

Silver's coat began to turn from brightness to rust and his body was scarred from battering against the rocks in his continual attempts to overcome the great barrier in his way. His strength grew less with every attempt, but the light in his eyes burnt more fiercely than ever, and the brave old heart within him was still undaunted. He was Silver, King of the River, mightiest of salmon; he wished to spawn, and he would spawn. Once more he leaped, only to fall back bruised and battered upon the naked rocks. He was mad with anger and utterly reckless, for he knew that, however bright the fires inside him might be, his strength was dying. He must have known, too, that there was no other way to the Spawning Beds; but after each unsuccessful attempt at the falls Silver circled the pool, keeping close to the rock-bound sides, turning back from the outlet that led to the sea, passing and repassing the salmon ladder, so despised in the days of his strength, which now stood high and dry above the sunken level of the pool, the white concrete of its steps weathered by the past few years. And each completed circle brought him back to the deep water at the foot of the falls, to another gallant attempt to leap clear over the six-foot wall of rock.

Then the Good Fisherman came down to the pool. He came without his rod, for he had been away some time, and had only walked down just "to have a look at things" and see if the water was really as low as he had been told it was.

He walked straight down to the edge of the pool, and stood for some time with his hands in his pockets, gazing dismally at the mere trickle of water that was coming over the falls. He turned to look downstream an instant, and Silver chose that instant to make a leap at the falls. The Good Fisherman was not quick enough to see the whole thing, but the echoes of the mighty splash were still playing among the rocks as he stared at the rings widening across the face of the pool, and he wondered at the madness of the fish that had made that leap. Silver was quite unconscious of the fact that he was observed, and even if he had known it he would not have cared. He lay on the bottom with fury in his heart, amazed at the discovery of an obstacle that dared stand in his way. Slowly his strength returned, until he was ready for one more attempt. He summoned all the power of his steel muscles, all the speed hidden in his tail and fins and body, and leaped again. He struck the top of the fall, he was almost over, but there was no water to give resistance to that last flick of the tail that forces a salmon up through the current and over the falls. He slipped back down the rocks and into the pool again.

The Good Fisherman had missed nothing this time, and his eyes shone with admiration for a gallant heart and with a fisherman's delight in a glimpse of the fish of his dreams. He saw that Silver would never reach the Spawning-Beds, and his thoughts turned at once to find the best method of catching him. Like all good fishermen, his first aim was to learn what must be Silver's state of mind. Under normal conditions it would have been waste of time to try for any fish with the River as low as it was, but the Good Fisherman understood a great deal about salmon. He knew that no salmon would attempt that leap under normal conditions, and he guessed at the anger that must be flaring in Silver's brain.

It was early in the afternoon of the next day when the Good Fisherman returned to the pool, bringing with him two rods—one a twelve-foot fly rod, and the other a very light spinning rod. He set to work at once with the fly rod, keeping well out of sight and working a tiny fly across and across. Twice he changed the fly and refished the pool, and at last he was rewarded. Silver had been aware of the first two flies, but had made no move. As the third fly swung over him he moved slightly—ever so slightly, but enough to disclose his position to the trained and watchful eyes of the Good Fisherman. The next fly that danced across the pool was a size larger, and it travelled quite two feet below the surface. Four times it passed above him, and Silver grew angry. It came once more, and Silver swam at it in fury, turned and struck it with his broad tail.

The Good Fisherman smiled, and his fingers trembled as he picked up the other rod and fixed a tiny red prawn to a delicate hook. He moved back to his position on the bank, crouching very low; then the prawn flew out and landed without a splash close under the far bank. Slowly the fisherman reeled in, and the prawn wobbled two yards in front of Silver's nose. Another cast, and it was only a yard from Silver's nose. Sixty pounds of salmon quivered with fury. Another cast, and this time the prawn passed so close to him that Silver drew back with a restless movement. Once again the faintest flash under the water told the Good Fisherman what had happened, and once again he smiled. He glanced at the watch on his wrist, and for ten long minutes he knelt without a move. Then he made another cast, even more delicate and accurate than the others. Ever so slowly the tiny prawn wobbled across, almost touching the River-bed. It drew closer to Silver, moving with maddening slowness. It passed him, just behind his tail—and like a flash the great fish had turned and seized it in his jaws. The Good Fisherman's hand trembled again, but he waited a moment before he struck and felt the hook go well home.

There was a tiny pause, while the pain shot from Silver's jaw to his brain; then the rod was almost torn from the fisherman's grasp.

Straight down the pool went Silver, and turned like a hard-pressed hare on the plough as he came to the shallows. Back to the falls, down again to the shallows, then straight to the fisherman's feet. For five minutes he fought at tremendous speed, running and jumping and rolling. Then he felt that his strength was failing fast, and he turned to sullen, heavy tactics.

Silver shook his head fiercely, he turned and twisted his body, he slapped the line with his tail and he tried to roll it round him. It was no good, for the fisherman never gave him one second of rest or one inch more line than he had to. For two long hours they fought, and the trickle of water over the fall was tinged with red from the setting sun before Silver knew that he was looking death in the face at last. His body was almost dead already, but the heart still lived, and it heard a last call to

the Spawning-Beds. Fighting for line with sullen plunges, Silver swam to the tail of the pool. He turned slowly, with his great back out of the water; then he dived and sped up towards the falls, deep down, near the bottom of the pool. It was a glorious rush, quite beyond the control of any fisherman, and it ended with the most glorious leap that a hooked salmon has ever made, straight for the top of the falls. For a moment it seemed that he was over, but inch by inch he was forced back till he fell, and the fight was finished. Silver lay on his side without a move as the fisherman reeled him in, and when he was lifted from the water he was quite dead. The Good Fisherman knelt beside his capture to read the mark on that silly little fin near the great broad tail, and he saw the scar of the poacher's spear.

What the Good Fisherman thought or said as he looked at the battered glory that had been Silver and thought of the wonderful heart of the great fish, I do not know. But his hands were very clumsy as he sought to remove the hook from Silver's jaw, and his eyes were rather sad when he turned uphill towards the lodge.